Unstoppable Money:
A Little Book About
Big Money

Unstoppable Money:
A Little Book About Big Money

Duane Marino

Prominent Books

ISBN 10: 194238906X

ISBN 13: 978-1-942389-06-4

Published by Prominent Books, LLC

Prominent Books and the Prominent Books
logo are property of Prominent Books, LLC.

TABLE OF CONTENTS

Live in Style, Retire in Comfort

These are your simple no-risk steps to guaranteed independent financial freedom for the average Joe and Josephine.

What your accountant and financial advisors don't know or won't tell you....

Introduction

I have worked with almost 50,000 people up to this point, and believe me, success and failure leave clues. When I start a personal coaching relationship with a client, one of my favorite questions to ask is, "When you play sports, gamble, compete in business, or work on the game of life, what is the biggest motivator for you—do you love to win, or do you hate to lose?" Check in with your head, heart, and gut right now, and determine which one drives you the most.

If you love to win, you are probably a eustress and pleasure seeker, need continually higher highs to get the endorphin rush that you love to feel, are driven by a very active limbic mind, and are typically a risk taker.

If you hate to lose, you are likely a distress and pain avoider, do whatever you can to avoid the cortisol rush that you hate to feel, are driven by a very active amygdala, are typically risk-averse, and are drawn towards security.

I can tell you from personal experience, when it comes to money, knowing which one you are can save you years of frustration.

In my other book *Unstoppable Selling*, I point out many things that will easily help any business person or salesperson become more successful. Over decades, I have unpacked sales strategies from the most successful people I could find, personally modeled what they did while I was selling, proved to myself and others that it worked, and then packaged up the techniques to create my own unique selling and teaching style. The same holds true with my money, and here with *Unstoppable Money*.

Many of you reading this small but powerful book are (or hopefully will be) wealthier than me. Unlike so many other books on money, which I found were just brainwashing sales tools for money market investment firms, this book shows you the very real and simple mechanics and street psychology of what all your rich friends know but don't tell you. Or if you are already rich, this book covers what you have probably figured out but (maybe) don't share!

I learned a long time ago that making money and cash flow are important, but what you do with that money is crucial. As an entrepreneur and salesperson, by the time I was in my mid-30s, I had a modest 7-figure net worth. Then came the 2008 market crash. My business stood still for almost 2 years while my expenses carried on. I took a 6-figure hit on the money markets. I watched my personal and business debt start to creep up and saw just how precarious my financial position was. I saw peers lose their businesses, their money, their families, and a few almost lost their minds.

While in the midst of that shake-up, I had the time and motivation to read a lot of books and attend a lot of workshops about money and started to pay very close attention to the people around me who were not experiencing the pain I was. I began to notice patterns I had not really paid attention to before.

There was one quote in Robert Kiyosaki's book *Conspiracies of the Rich* that really resonated with me and hit me like a hammer on my head. He talked about the lifestyles and money habits of his two fathers and said that when he was younger, his "rich dad wasn't rich yet, and his poor dad wasn't poor yet." In fact, the dad who lived rich ended up broke, and the dad who lived poorly ended up rich.

Ironically, in my life, I was watching exactly that happen. The skills, habits and attitudes towards wealth and lifestyle were leading some people in my life to financial ruin and others to success. It was right in front of my nose. I realized I was at a crossroads and needed to start making even better choices.

To make a long story short, that downturn was one of the best things to ever happen to me and my money. It made me analyze and cultivate new money strategies, create a new story about who I am, and want to really be financially stable. And it challenged my ability to manage my state of mind and emotions through it all.

Anyone can let the good times roll, but it's when conditions turn down that your character and capacity are really tested.

This book is short for a reason: complexity is the enemy of execution, financial success is easy, and it is all within your control. If you execute the concepts laid out in the next few pages, your financial future will be very, very bright.

I promise you will win more and lose less. Like everything else I teach, I know this because I have and do live it.

I hope you enjoy and profit from *Unstoppable Money*!

How to Retire in Comfort

At the conclusion of each section is a worksheet you must complete.

These plans will bring you a sense of excitement and peace with an exact and realistic program that you have 100% control over. You will see that, regardless of your current income, you can attain wealth mastery.

This book may be small, but massive things can come in tiny packages. For example, the "Law of Gravity" has only three words, but disregarding them can have big implications.

Just pay attention to the following "**6 P's**", master using "**PAASSCDTT**" in your everyday life, and complete and live by your **worksheets**!

The 6 P's

Principles: there are laws of obtaining and sustaining your financial health, as sure as the law of gravity, that you need to understand to be able to apply the...

Practices: using simple and proven methods that anyone can take advantage of if you follow strong...

Psychology: to improve your financial future, you have to start thinking like someone who is already in a great financial position and stay in good mental, emotional, spiritual, and physical shape so you can enjoy your money. To move from a consumer to an investor, watch for the…

Patterns: the things that you do on a daily basis that increase or decrease your…

Probability: of you being financially free and creating a life that is…

Predictable: because success or failure is not the result of luck!

Nobody cares as much about your money as you, so don't give all the keys to your financial future to your broker (who may be broker than you), your "bank-ster" who simply wants to control your money, and stop watching the paid talking heads on TV's corporate "bad-news" shows and reading papers that are written by "press-titutes" who are paid to push someone else's fear-based agendas on you!

So, if you can be open-minded but skeptical, without fear or ego, you are ready to start your new financial future! Buckle up; here we go....

Wealth Health Laws of PAASSCDTT

I have an acronym I suggest you tattoo to your forearm (or put on your fridge.) It is called "PAASSCDTT". Your financial health depends on you understanding and obeying this, so meditate on PAASSCDTT regularly. Understanding and living by the laws of PAASSCDTT will mean the difference between your financial slavery and your financial freedom. I can promise you that your rich friends obey the laws of PAASSCDTT and your broke friends break them regularly.

You need to work on these areas

simultaneously, but the reverse order of PAASSCDTT, as it is written below, is the order in which you must master and tackle it.

T – Taxes. Pay yourself second and the government first! Learn how to legally and ethically pay as little tax as possible, but ALWAYS pay ALL your taxes, and pay them on time; failure to do so will result in stress, insolvency, and possible jail time. Keep meticulous tax records for possible future use.

T – Time. The sooner you start this entire plan, the sooner you will be financially free.

D – Debt. There is a difference between good and bad debt. Going into debt and paying interest for things that depreciate (e.g. anything you buy at a mall on credit cards) or cost money to own is bad. Going into debt for things that will appreciate or generate more money than the debt costs is good (such as most property or a successful business). Your strategy for becoming debt-free in five years or less is near the back of this book.

C – Credit. Being able to go into good debt is affected by your cash position, credit rating, and how much confidence lenders have in you. Google and YouTube "What affects my beacon/FICO score" and "Understanding my credit report".

Information is potential power. Your money also wants you to stay single or not divorce if you're already married.

S – Spending. Your household needs to keep a journal of where money is spent so everyone is aware of their daily decisions. This single action will allow you to keep your eyes on your money every day.

S – Savings. Once you have a grip on your bad debt and on your spending, you can focus on your savings. Cash is king. In my opinion, you should keep all your bank assets, such as deposits, at a different institution than your debts (this also includes anything you may have stored in a safety deposit box.) This will prevent your bank from causing irreparable harm or instantly wiping you out using their legal right of offset that you probably agreed to in all your banking documents. This right allows them to pay down or pay off any of your debts, without warning or cause, using any and all assets held within that institution. I have seen many naive people become permanently damaged financially by not understanding this.

A – Active Income. Make lots of hay while the sun shines. Maximize your income earning potential while you still feel like working, or are able to.

A – Assets. Accumulate high quality assets. **Great** assets go up in value AND throw off cash (e.g. income property). **Good** assets go up/hold relative value OR throw off cash (e.g.

metals, antiques, land or even busy vending machines). **<u>Bad</u>** assets go down in value OR cost you money to own (e.g. all consumer goods). And **<u>terrible</u>** assets go down in value AND continually require cash (e.g. average vehicles are transportation, not investments).

P – Passive Income … Welcome to financial Nirvana. Eventually you won't want to work, or won't be able to, but you will need a source of cash flow or income. The most reliable ways to achieve this are through income property, a pension (but if you quit, get fired or are laid off, they reduce plans or close their doors—it's gone, so don't bank on it) or a business you own that can operate profitably without you. I wouldn't count on the money markets for this one, as you may not have the time to ride the storm if the market tanks when you want to retire. (The formula for acquiring income properties is toward the end of this book.)

Pondering, understanding, and living by the laws of PAASSCDTT is a logical, safe, and easy way to understand, create, and preserve your wealth health. The question is, will you be able to "PAASSCDTT" the test one day?

.

Executing the following diversified, simple steps will allow you to retire soon, at your current lifestyle, as your contributions are always scaled proportionally to your current situation.

Put Life Insurance on Your Parents

I didn't have the opportunity to take advantage of this. At first, I found this distasteful, but as I found out, several cultures (with money coincidentally) do this the day their baby is born. The parents purchase it for the child, with the child being the beneficiary. If you are like me and weren't so lucky to come from one of those families, be practical and do it today. Logically, and unfortunately, your parents or parent will never be younger or be in better health than today, so their premiums will only go up from here, and the amount of insurance they qualify for will only go down.

Do your research, and call several insurance companies for quotes and terms. Buy as much as you can afford for the highest payoff possible. Maybe your parents are able or willing to pay half of your premiums so you can buy twice as much. If your parents aren't available or don't qualify for this, you could possibly find someone who is at the very least 25 years older than you, and ask them if you can insure against their death with you as the beneficiary, if allowed by your carrier. (I know of some unscrupulous people who befriend and endear senior citizens just to become their executors or get in their wills! I am not advocating this!) Even if you have a legitimate connection, this aspect of financial planning may seem taboo to some people, but it is a very smart and practical move. Do this today for whatever amount you can afford, and continue to increase that insurance in the future if you wish.

When the unfortunate circumstances take place that trigger this pay out, you will use that cash to fund your increase in more great assets. And while we are on the topic of insurance, when was the last time you did a full review of your own personal and professional coverages to protect you and your family from a catastrophic loss of income due to disability, medical bills, or death? Inadequate insurance protection on a household's primary income earner(s) health is a major cause of financial failure. Take a peak at PAASSCDTT if you aren't sure how to pay for this.

Your Plan: Your parents (or surrogates) are now ___ years old. I will discuss this practical financial plan with them. Upon their authorization, I will acquire life insurance on them for the most I can afford.

Using the laws of PAASSCDTT, this aspect of my financial planning will require a monthly investment of $_____ and with a future payoff of $_____.

Signed:_____
Dated:_____

Live off 85% of Your Income

Starting the day you read this, create an automatic electronic withdrawal that moves 15% of every paycheck into a different bank account. You will never miss that money because it never lands in your account. This will stop you from spending all your money, or worse yet, living beyond your means. You don't touch that money until the day you stop working. Just trick yourself into thinking you make 15% less, no matter if your pay goes up or down. Ideally, it's an interest earning savings account that is in another city, at a different banking institution, and does not have check writing, debit card or electronic banking privileges. So if the urge strikes you to touch that money, you have to physically drive there to get it and will hopefully sober up and realize how foolish that would be for your financial future, and you turn around and go home.

Reader, refer to PAASSCDTT in the previous section to figure out what to do with your 85%. By the way, if your income was $100,000 and you only put away 10%, that's $10,000; but if you put away 15%, that's $15,000. In real terms, that's just a 5% difference today, but a 50% increase in total savings tomorrow! And that is a game changer for your future.

Your Plan: Using the laws of PAASSCDTT, my after-tax net income is $_____$ per year, 15% of which is $_____$.

My retirement forecast is that in ___ years, I will be ___ years old and will have tucked away $_____$ not including interest.

Using __% as a very conservative compound interest rate, this will accumulate into total cash savings of about $_____$.

I will open an interest-bearing savings account at an inaccessible location and begin putting away 15% of my net earnings. I won't touch that money until I stop working.

Signed:_____

Dated:_____

Buy Your Home & Pay it off Fast

Historically, over time, property is one of your best bets, and its value is always relative to the local cost of living. Don't live in too much home that takes all your earning power to sustain, because a home is not a great asset. It usually appreciates over time, but it costs money to operate, and to get your money out of it, you have to sell or mortgage it and will still need a place to live.

The only thing stopping you from owning your home is adhering to the laws of PAASSCDTT. Paying it off quickly through accelerated payments, pre-payments, or shortening the term will save you enormous amounts of money in interest, reduce the time it takes you to start the next idea, and give you huge satisfaction. I don't really recommend it, but the only reason you would ever touch your 15% savings from the previous idea is for the down payment on your first home, allowing you to get into the property ownership game quickly.

When you rent, you are buying your landlord's property for them, increasing their wealth health and deteriorating yours. A good guideline is that the maximum total monthly outlay for your home is around 25% of your gross annual income. So a person netting $50,000 a year would be looking at about $12,500 a year, or just over $1000 a month, going towards principal, interest and taxes to carry it. Assuming a $25,000 down payment (which would take just over 3 years to save using your 15% savings) you could purchase about a $200,000-ish property. Adjust all these numbers in accordance with your income and carrying terms. Welcome home, soldier!

Your Plan: I will adhere to the laws of PAASSCDTT so that I can acquire a good asset such as my home.

I will save $_____ per month for ____ months so that I can purchase a home for about $_____ in value by approximately the month of _____ in 20__ and have it paid off in ____ years, or about the year 20__.

Signed:_____
Dated:_____

Get an Income Property

If you are risk and debt-averse, you can wait to buy your first income property as soon as you pay off your home. You could do it sooner when you develop enough equity in your home to allow you to leverage it and borrow against it for the down payment of your income property (probably tax-free), and then work towards paying off your newly acquired small mortgage on your home quickly. This second property is now a great asset (the laws of PAASSCDTT) that will eventually increase in value with decreasing debt and throw off cash.

By paying your rent, your renter is making the principal, interest and property tax payments on your income property and essentially buying your property for you. You can leverage and borrow against this great asset down the road to buy more great assets or withdraw money from the equity accumulated in it (probably tax-free).

Your Plan: By obeying the laws of PAASSCDTT, I will have my home paid off or paid down by the month of _____ 20__, which will allow me to leverage it for the down payment of my first income property, which is a great asset.

This property will be valued at about $_____ and will be paid off by my tenants.

I will pay off that newly acquired small mortgage on my home by the month of _____ 20__. At that time, I will decide to create more wealth or just preserve what I have built.

Signed:_____

Dated:_____

Predict Your Future!

Add together the above final values for plans 1-4:

1. _____ + 2. _____

+ 3. _____ + 4. _____

= $_____.

If I divide the total above of $_____ by the number of years I anticipate needing an income after retirement (_____ years), I will have control over a cash flow of $_____ per year. This is assuming you have cashed out all of the above investments and are not generating any return on that money at all, which is highly unlikely. So this is a worst-case scenario prediction. You have planned your work, now just work your plan! BAM!

Bonus Debt Elimination Plan

Reader, if you and everyone else in your household commits to this plan, you will be debt-free within 5 years. If I did it, you can do it too! The joy and freedom you will get from this cannot be expressed in words. Instead of making it a chore, we turned this into a game. And instead of it being painful, it became fun.

Remember, ¾ of success is psychology! Once you decide that the pain of discipline is better than the pain of regret, this program is a no-brainer. Remember, any interest you don't pay over time is money that goes straight into your net worth today. Here is the strategy:

1.   Maintain a household journal to record where ALL money is being spent, every last cent, every day. Complete it at the end of each day. The awareness this brings to your money habits is truly priceless.

2.   Commit to only paying cash for all purchases while you are on this program of debt elimination. Do not keep more than $20 in your pocket at a time, and see how many days you can go without spending it.

3.   Before you spend a dime, ask yourself, *If I don't buy this, will my*

life or the life of someone I love come to an end? If not, don't buy it.

4.   When spending money on anything you determine to be a necessity, ask yourself, *Is there a less expensive way to do or get this?*

5.   Continue to invest in your own learning, business, and marketing only on things you feel you can get at least a 10:1 return on your investment. You are your best asset, so keep investing in yourself wisely.

6.   Make as much money as you can, working your butt off and taking massive action on all things related to increasing your cash flow.

7.   Learn your local tax laws,

maximize every opportunity to pay as little tax as possible, and make paying your taxes in full, on time, your number-one priority.

8.   You will start to notice a huge positive gap between what you are bringing in and what is going out. Now take all this extra cash flow you are generating and pay off any past due taxes first if applicable, then your smallest debt. Once that debt is paid, do not incur any more debt in that area, and pay your next smallest debt. The extra cash flow you are now also creating from not having to service those debts gets dumped onto your next biggest debt, and so on. The positive domino effect this creates is extremely exciting.

9.   In a very short time, you will be plowing so much cash onto your final remaining debt, while not incurring any more debt, that you will shock yourself as to how fast you will become debt free. Remember that the word "mortgage" literally means "deathgrip"!

Extra Bonus: Income Property Accumulation

Look around. I would bet almost everyone you know who has acquired real wealth health has done it through income properties! Here is a very simple formula you and I can use to create financial security and freedom by buying and holding onto income properties:

It's important that you understand your local lender's loan to value guidelines. This needs to be established before your first purchase so that you can use the appropriate math.

In a few pages, I will walk you through a real-life example of a small single-family home income property I recently completed. At that time, the lender's guidelines allowed for up to 80% of the value to be financed. This number will vary based on lender, market conditions, type and size of property. Do your homework before you buy to save yourself unnecessary hold ups and headaches.

1.   You will need the time to create and manage each project, the skills to refurbish and maintain them and the money to fund them. If you don't possess all three attributes, find like-minded partners who have the needed talents. *Partner right.*

2.   Start small and look for a run-down property in a highly rentable location on a nice street, close to public transportation and near schools. *Hunt right.*

3.   Your target investment should be structurally sound but in need of a major interior and exterior facelift. You want to purchase the property for no more than 60% of what the value will be after your renovations. *Buy right.*

4.   Use your cash or private lenders to fund the initial purchase. This solves the head ache of trying to get a prime lender to issue you a mortgage on a dilapidated property (which they won't) and then go back to your primary lender and ask for

substantially more money after your value-building renovations, which can cause more headaches. The new mortgage is what you will use to pay back your private lender and your construction costs. *Borrow right.*

5.	After you buy the property, work to finish the refurbishing quickly. You want to complete all the work, refinance it, pull out your initial investment, and rent it ASAP. Your investment costs for the renovations should ideally be no more than 20% of what the value will be after your renovations, so that after the purchase and renovations, your total investment does not exceed 80% of the final value. You only want to renovate this property once, so pay special attention to things like the roof, furnace, water heater, wiring, plumbing, landscaping, kitchen, bathrooms, and living areas. Your inspection before purchase should have detailed the items and costs of your anticipated renovations. Use materials and workmanship that will last a long time, such as ceramics, laminate floors, durable trim and composite kitchens, with the idea in mind that when renters turn over, all you will have to do is a deep cleaning and maybe some painting. Good renters are easy to find if you have a nice property that holds up over time. *Renovate right.*

6. As soon as the renovations are complete, contact your primary

lender(s) and have them appraise your now beautiful property for the first time, and seek enough funds to pay off all or the majority of your renovation costs. *Refinance right.*

7.   Be patient and selective when choosing tenants. Call references, drive by where they used to live, call employers, join a landlord community that will advise you on your local rental services and laws, be clear on expectations regarding upkeep, grass cutting, garbage, snow removal, pets, etc. *Rent right.*

8.   Hold your investment for the long term. This great asset is now controlled and owned by you. You have little-to-none of your own money in it, your tenants will be

paying your mortgage and buying it for you, you can borrow against it or pull cash out of it in later years, and it will appreciate in value and eventually throw off cash every month. *Own right.*

Take out a scratch pad, and follow me in one real-life example:

Through a friend in real estate, we found a small single-family home with potential curb appeal in an older but nice neighborhood near public transportation and schools. It was just going under a power of sale due to back taxes and mortgage payment delinquency.

Upon inspection of the house, it

was structurally sound but was completely trashed on the inside and totally ignored on the outside.

The market assessment of nearby properties showed it should be worth about $200,000 after the renovations. We purchased it for just over $100,000 using a short-term fixed payment open loan from a private investor. We poured $50,000 of renovations into it, turning it into the nicest property on the street both in and out in 90 days.

After 90 days, we sought appraisals and standard financing from prime lenders and at the same time listed the house for rent.

The banks loved the house and assessed the value at just under

$200,000 in it's current condition and approved a mortgage of 80% of it's value, or about $160,000.

After the advance of $160,000, we paid off the private lender their $100,000, recouped our construction costs of about $50,000, and the property now stood with zero financial investment from us.

We rented it to a high-quality tenant and are holding it.

Relax when looking for your properties, as new things are always coming on the market, and opportunities are always changing. So be patient as the deal of a lifetime is often just two weeks away. And take the same approach when screening potential tenants. If you have the right unit, be diligent as the tenant of the decade can be just two days away. Never buy or rent out of fear of loss.

Duane Brain Tip: start researching where to retire by joining websites, online communities, newsletters, and magazine subscriptions devoted to the research of exactly that! Hundreds of experts devote a lot of time and money into passing on their experiences. There are many safe, clean and comfortable countries with outstanding health care, amenities, and climates that you can retire in for a fraction of the cost of where you currently live. This can substantially change the standards, cost, and time frame of your retirement plan!

Conclusion:

Reader, make the decision to start managing your own future today and stop leaving it up to the "experts" who make it seem like it's too difficult or confusing for you to do on your own. Meditation and wishful thinking will only go so far. I hope you take action.

Talk to your accountant and tax planner regarding the local laws and tax trends that might affect your personal situation and plan. Don't let fear, habits or laziness stop you! Start this today! And avoid negativity at all costs!

The information in this book has

worked for me and countless others, so I know it will work for you too!

Head down, horns out and straight ahead!

Easy-peasy! Now, using discipline, desire, dedication, and determination … go secure your future! Do the math. This is a no-fail plan that you control.

About the Author

Duane Marino is an independent entrepreneur and strategist. As we all strive for continuous improvement, his passion is helping people with maximization of their potential.

Duane believes this is accomplished by exercising honest reflection while moving towards new goals and never letting fear, bad habits, or complacency slow one's progress.

Duane's overall goal is to always leave things better than the way he found them through certain maxims, perspectives, and ways of interaction that include, in part, the following:

- Life and business require that we make contact with others during the regular course of each day. In this small world, every point of contact must have a clear and straightforward intention with outcomes as positive as possible.

- You must be careful not to let your strengths become weaknesses.

- Often, the qualities that contribute to initial greatness are the same ones that lead to eventual failure.

Self-awareness is everything. Without exception, Duane has personally experienced, applied, and executed all of the information he teaches.

With regard to wealth, it is not about how much money you make but how much you keep and who else can benefit along the way while you build wealth.

Unstoppable Money is the logical sequel to Duane's #1 best-seller, *The Six Sales Powers to Unstoppable Selling*—ISBN: 978-1942389040, Prominent Books, LLC. Duane lives by the principles, practices, psychology, and patterns in both books.

For more information on Mr. Marino's coaching, feel free to contact him at: www.DuaneMarino.com or email: info@DuaneMarino.com.